Twelve Years of Christmas

✳

Books by *Rod McKuen*

Poetry:
And Autumn Came

Stanyan Street and Other Sorrows

Listen to the Warm

Lonesome Cities

Twelve Years of Christmas

In Someone's Shadow

Caught in the Quiet

A Man Alone (Privately Printed)

With Love . . .

Fields of Wonder

The Carols of Christmas

Moment to Moment

Collected Lyrics:
New Ballads

Pastorale

Grande Tour

Rod McKuen

Twelve
Years
of Christmas

W. H. Allen · London & New York
A division of Howard & Wyndham Ltd.

For Nan and Gay
and my Mother

Author's Note

The poems collected here were never meant
to be a book. Each was a Christmas card
written for my friends year by year.

Going through these pages I've discovered
that Christmas was not always a celebration
for me, it was more a time of summing up.

Each December for eleven years my friends
have had a poem from me. This book holds
number twelve, for Katie.

Rod McKuen,
1969

Contents

Nineteen fifty-eight

The Counterpoint of Carols

Now softly come the minstrels
    heads bowed into hymnals
  caroling for cookies and safe smiles.
We owe them more than candy
for the redness of their ears alone.

Faint footsteps down the hill and gone,
there music dying through the trees
as back to Bach we go
        on phonographs and radios.

The needlepoint of patchwork quilts,
the counterpoint of carols.

Novembers come and gone too soon
there are so many quarrels
that we haven't finished,
and they might lessen
                in the January rain.

Quarrel in December?
   Never.
November comes up every year.
This Christmas comes but once.

I am not master of the holly,
nor are you mistress to the fire.
Still, together we're the Christmas people
and dancing down the year end has its merits.

We can fire our memories as the Yule logs burn
            and give away our secrets
         each in turn.

Never mind what Whitman said,
proud music of the storm never kept the
nations quiet;
lovers each to each do that —
they know that wars don't work
forever.

Merry then and *Allelulah* too,
I love you just as much as I love Christ.
No.
More.
He opened up my life for me.
You unlocked the final door.

Nineteen
fifty-nine

*

True Holly

Because I love the sound of bells
I haunt the churchyards all year long
no matter where I might be travelling.

Because true holly makes me smile
I wait for Christmas just like children,
And I wait for children too.

Because September travels slow
I catch it when I can
and hold it over for another month or two.

Because this year I'm poor again
I've written you another Christmas poem
made with last year's love and next year's too.

Nineteen
sixty

The Jazz Palace

I have never been to Disneyland
                    Freedomland or Roseland.
I waste my time looking under subway
                                        cushions,
between the popcorn and the gum,
                    for pennies,
or going to the movies
and later eating hot dogs
at Grants on Forty-second Street.

Sometimes in penny arcades I take my picture —
                    four for a quarter.
Rock Hudson isn't worried, or the camera lies
(I saw him yesterday in *Taza Son of Cochise*).
Later I tore up my arcade pictures, one by one.
Even those that made me look
                    like Robert Mitchum's son.

I get up early when the movies change
and so I'm on a first-name basis
with a certain cleaning lady at *The Times*.
(Years later Mr Atkinson may write about
     this special friendship,
but how am I to know these things
at such a tender age?)

Some days near Sutton Place
                    down by the river
I watch the tugs not tugging only passing by.
But it's the movies I like best
          except the one called *Wild Heritage*.

I have seen *No Man's Woman* thirteen times.
One day I will buy The Jazz Palace for Marie
                              Windsor.

Nineteen sixty-one

*

*

Christmas with the Masses

I spent Christmas with a cinder in my eye,
watching a priest eat a hot dog on Sixth
                                    Avenue
                    between masses.

Fifth had store windows
with imitation trees and imitation holly
and imitation women walked on the arms
of men with imitation smiles.

My mother gave me five saints' names
            in hopes I'd be protected
but the enemy's so silent
I wouldn't know him if he came.

Smitten by the robber or the robber's smile
            I'd most likely turn the other
                                cheek.

Like hell I would.

But forgive me my trespasses
        they've been few this year
(unless you count the time
I crossed Sixth Avenue against the light
in order that I might be blessed
between the mustard and the relish).

for Barbara

Nineteen sixty-two

Another Thank You

Thank you
for kissing me in the elevator last night.

Holidays meant little when I was young,
only supper at separate tables from the
grown-ups.

So thank you for the flowers and the snow
this morning
and for jam from the delicatessen
and for loving me.

Thank you for this one-room world.
    (All I need
                when you're here.)

Today while lying face to face
with love again
I closed my eyes to seasons and to skies
and I was younger than I've ever been.

            Thank you.

Nineteen sixty-three

*

Tomorrow

I know that love is running in the snow.
I cannot see it but it's there.
As sure as caterpillars tunnel in the leaves
and winter weight bogs down the trees.

And so I search the highways and the hills.

                    There was a time
when bar talk and Bartok did the job
and I would hurry home —
          a stranger in my arms or in my
                                        thoughts
to be content with San Francisco rain.

You'd be surprised
the way the dripping rain from rooftops
can ease a man from out himself
                              and into sun.

We're all older now.
This past year we have lost Piaf's smile,
                              Kennedy's promises
and Cocteau's jokes on everyone
(he said the ship was going down—
                              remember).

The year turns home.

Maybe tomorrow.

for Ed Habib

Nineteen
sixty-four

Saving Things

I save things.
Kites, coloured rocks
and people's smiles
twine and sea shells
Jacques Brel records and words.
There are some things I've kept so long
I can't remember where they came from,
and certain souvenirs so new
I dare not watch them yet.

I have some marbles in a box
that played with me when I was nine.
The memory of a friend in France
who said to me one day
Je suis fort mais j'aime les roses
then went away.

In Spain this year
I wrote a song no one will ever sing,
I'll keep that too
along with rings and strings
                    and other things.

The worlds I used to know
are in my pocket
                or in my mind
behind the things I'm thinking now.

Hang the holly, trim the tree
Spain and Stanyan Street are miles away
and if I'm still alone this year
my mind is overflowing
with the things I've saved.

Nineteen
sixty-five

Naming the Baby

What a name to give a newborn child
                    Jesus.
Don't they know
he'll have to wear it all his life?

Bill or Robert would be easier to carry
through the years and up that final hill.
A man named Jesus has a saddle on him
from the first day on.

They might as well have called him Marvin
                    or Jean-Claude.
Whoever heard of Frank or Fred being
                    strung out on a cross.
Mothers never think of things like that.

How many kids named Elvis
               will grow up wondering?

A man needs all the help there is
               in later life,
just to stay anonymous in crowds.

Don't our fathers know
a man named Jesus or René
will draw K.P. because he sticks out
                    from the rest?

Those of us who wanted to
would still have known him from the other
                           Jims
Those of us who needed gentlemen
               would still have found him out.

Nineteen sixty-six

Pour Mon Cheval

At times I feel
there'll be no summer any more
that time of reason will not come again
and so I have my green days filed away
to call back when the snows come down.

There was the year I first heard Brel
               and cried
because I thought I'd never sing that well.
I took home sugar in those days
               pour mon cheval
and lived my life in St Germain cafés
and thought I liked Chagall.

How many summers gone,
        how many old days past,
how many July afternoons are never
                        coming back?

The snow falls now all bed-sheet white
the green days this year are all done.
I still go home with sugar
but when I fall asleep at night
I find my horse has run away and gone.

If summer comes again
will it be this year's Christmas I call back
to save me from the sun?

for all of them

Nineteen
sixty-seven

El Monte

I probably will never see El Monte on a
                                        Sunday
or El Segundo washed by winter rain.
I never knew these towns existed — if they do,
outside of the obituary page that states
how many boys came home today in boxes
                                        made of steel.

I'm well aware that some have died from
                                        Chicago too
but it's the new El Nowhere towns
            I think about this morning
and young men that the whole town knew.

Today some children running down the hill
            were shouting out *the war*
                        is over.
They must have had some private war of
                        words in mind.
Not the one I'm paying for
the one that's killing off the boys I see on
                        airplane rides
staring into space in search of El Dorado.
Sometimes I ask them where they're from,
El Paso is the answer or El Monte.

And so they take the tinsel from our lives
on airplane rides across the sea
and like the silver in our dimes
it won't come back
            until we question *why*.

El Monte's just ten minutes from L.A.
to some I'm told
it seems like El Dorado when it rains.

Just the same
            I doubt I'll ever go there on a Sunday.

for Joyce

Nineteen sixty-eight

✳

Corners

I turn each corner still
hoping for the Virgin Mary to appear.
She'll be dressed in cardboard blue
the way she was in Sunday school
and stepping out in front of me
        she'll lead me through another town.

Afterward,
her many miracles
still bulging from that shopping bag of hope,
she'll leave me standing by myself and
                        wondering.

I know that love
        like radios and ripe bananas
is auctioned in the market place

and all things meant to last were made
pre-1940.
Still a man can smile while waiting for the
light to change
and hope the Virgin Mary on her busy rounds
will stop to drink strong coffee
on the English Common
or in a North Beach square.

Kennedy and King,
you had the means but not the time.
And though the Virgin Mary
is nothing but a dream
her hair is soft and silky in the night.

for Katie

Nineteen
sixty-nine

Barking at Shadows

As December reaches home
it takes the shadows all of Sunday morning
to complete their survey of the yard.
Only in the eyes you notice winter
    those eyes unsure
behind fast fading summerskin
that took four months to get just right.

What a happy time to be alive and running,
eating California sunshine.
It didn't fall into the sea in April after all.

July's a month I won't forget.
    If I do
I hope the summer drags me back to spring
and leaves me dangling there.

Today is smaller
Than I thought it might be
And going quickly.
I'm in no hurry to be told tomorrow's news
                        until tomorrow.

Where Katie is
her God knows best.
Christmas will be quieter this year.
Please let it pass by swiftly
but not so quickly that I might forget
how much I learned of love
because she passed
            down through my life.

About the Author

ROD MCKUEN was born in California and grew up in California, Nevada, Washington and Oregon. He has travelled extensively as a concert artist, a composer and a writer. Before becoming an author and composer, Mr McKuen worked as a laborer, radio disc jockey and newspaper columnist and as a psychological-warfare scriptwriter during the Korean War. In just over four years his books of poetry have sold in excess of seven million copies in hardcover, making him the best-selling poet not only of this age but probably of every other era as well. In addition, he is the composer of more than a thousand popular songs and his film scores include *The Prime of Miss Jean Brodie*, and *A Boy Named Charlie Brown* (both of which earned him Academy Award Nominations), *Scandalous John*, *Joanna* and, with Henry Mancini, *Me, Natalie*.

His major classical works, *Symphony #1*, *Concerto for Four Harpsichords and Orchestra* and *Concerto for Guitar and Orchestra*, have been performed by leading orchestras. In May of 1972 The Royal Philharmonic Orchestra in London premiered his *Piano Concerto #1* and his ballet suite *Childhood* at the Royal Albert Hall as part of their Silver Jubilee Anniversary.

Mr McKuen's hobbies include skiing, sailing, and driving, and he is currently finishing an extensive book about the sea. When not travelling, he lives at home in California in a rambling Spanish house with a menagerie of cats and four sheepdogs—Mr Kelly, Old Boot, Arthur and Mr Kelly, Jr.

Commencing with the fall 1972 publication in America of his book *And to each Season*, Mr McKuen will begin lightening his concert and recording schedule to devote more time to his writing and classical composing.